DEPRESSION

DEPRESSION

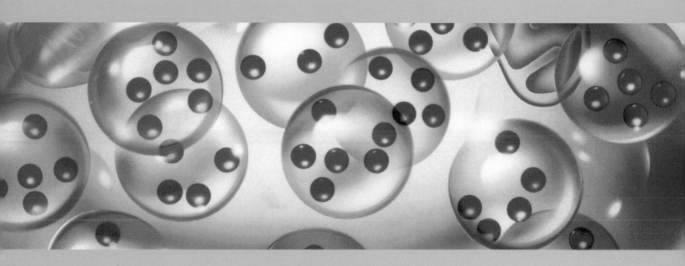

Jennifer Rozines Roy

BENCHMARK BOOKS

MARSHALL CAVENDISH
NEW YORK

Marshall Cavendish Benchmark
99 White Plains Road
Tarrytown, New York 10591-9001
www.marshallcavendish.us

This book is not intended for use as a substitute for advice, consultation, or treatment by a licensed medical practitioner. The reader is advised that no action of a medical nature should be taken without consultation with a licensed medical practitioner, including action that may seem to be indicated by the contents of this work, since individual circumstances vary and medical standards, knowledge, and practices change with time. The publisher, author, and medical consultants disclaim all liability and cannot be held responsible for any problems that may arise from use of this book.

Library of Congress Cataloging-in-Publication Data

Roy, Jennifer Rozines, 1967-
  Depression / by Jennifer Rozines Roy.
      p. cm. -- (Health alert)
  Includes bibliographical references and index.
  ISBN-13 978-0-7614-1800-9
  ISBN 0-7614-1800-8
  1. Depression, Mental--Juvenile literature. 2. Depression in adolescence--Juvenile literature. I. Title. II. Series:
Health alert (Benchmark Books)

  RC537.R69 2005
  616.85'27--dc22   2004005970

Front cover: A brain scan of a person suffering from depression
Title page: An illustration of neurotransmitters

Photo research by Regina Flanagan

Front cover: WDCN / Univ. College London / Photo Researchers, Inc.
The photographs in this book are used by permission and through the courtesy of: *Photo Researchers, Inc.*: John Bavosi, 4, 17; VVG, 5, 15; Jim Varney, 13, 43; Garry Watson, 20; WDCN / Univ. College London, 23; SPL, 24; Pascal Goetgheluck, 28; Cordelia Molloy, 29; National Library of Medicine, 33, 35; Geoff Tompkinson, 37; Peter Bowater, 38; Mark Clarke, 41; Leonard Lessin, Fbpa, 45; Will & Deni McIntyre, 53. *Corbis:* 19, 50, 51; Bettmann, 36; Jose Luis Pelaez, Inc., 46. *Picture Quest:* Creatas, 57.

Printed in China
6 5 4 3

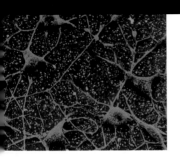

CONTENTS

1

WHAT IS DEPRESSION LIKE?

Tamyra's Story

Tamyra is thirteen years old. She loves to go bike riding and in-line skating with her friends. She is on the honor roll and sings in the school chorus. When she was growing up, Tamyra's mom called her "Sunshine" because she was so cheerful. Lately, however, her friends call her "Miss Moody."

Her friends have been asking her what is wrong. But Tamyra always answers, "Nothing." However, the truth is she does not feel like herself anymore. Some days she feels cranky. Other days she is tired and sad. She has been sleeping more than usual and has been eating a lot less than normal. Tamyra does not enjoy doing the things she usually likes to do. She has not gone biking or skating in months. She has also been thinking about quitting chorus because she just does not feel like singing.

Her friends tell her to snap out of it and to lighten up. Tamyra knows they are right. She thinks she should just get over it. But she cannot.

At school one day, Tamyra was called to the guidance counselor's office. She was surprised to see her parents sitting with her counselor and one of her teachers. Her teacher told Tamyra's parents that she was worried about her. Tamyra's grades have slipped, she had not handed in some assignments, and she sometimes fell asleep in class.

Tamyra's parents had also noticed that she seemed a little sad lately. But they thought that Tamyra was just having a rough time like most teenagers. They assumed that in time, Tamyra would go back to being happy. But Tamyra's counselor believed that Tamyra was suffering from depression—an illness that can affect people of all ages. At first, her parents did not believe it because they thought that only adults could suffer from depression. Soon after, however, they took her to a doctor to make sure that she was allright.

After running some tests and asking Tamyra a lot of questions, the doctor decided that Tamyra was suffering from depression. He instructed her to take special antidepressant medicine. As part of her treatment, Tamyra visited with the school **psychologist** (a person who studies the mind and the way people behave) once a week. They talked about how she was feeling, what was bothering her, and how to handle the different problems she might was having.

After two months, Tamyra was feeling a little better. After four months, she was biking and skating again. Her grades improved and she was singing in the school chorus again. Her friends noticed that the old happy Tamyra was back.

Depression is something that Tamyra will have to deal with for a long time, but she knows that she is not alone. She knows that millions of people across the country also suffer from depression and that there is nothing to be ashamed of.

Josh's Story

Josh is a healthy eleven-year-old boy. When he was five, his mother died in a car accident and since then, his dad has taken care of him. Josh and his dad usually get along well. They go to music concerts, hike, and ski together.

But a few weeks ago, Josh noticed his dad acting weird. At the dinner table, his dad talked quickly and excitedly about things that did not seem to make sense. He claimed to be inventing a secret machine that was going to change the world. Josh's dad had also been staying up late at night—sometimes not even sleeping at all—in order to work on a secret project.

One day his dad brought him to a mall and bought a lot of expensive clothes. Josh was happy to go shopping with his dad, but he did not know why they had to buy so much. He and his dad did not have a lot of money, so Josh did not know how they could afford all of the new stuff. But his dad was not worried about that. He told Josh they needed the clothes for when they became famous from the secret invention.

A few days later, Josh came home from school to find all of the new clothes scattered on the front lawn. His dad had thrown them out the window. When Josh tried to ask what was wrong, he found his dad lying in bed, looking sad and angry. He told Josh to go away and leave him alone. His dad would not even come downstairs to eat dinner. Josh did not know what to do, so he called his Uncle Jack. The next day, Uncle Jack took Josh's dad to see a **psychiatrist**—a doctor who studies the mind and the way people behave.

When his dad and uncle returned, they told Josh about his dad's disease. For many years, his father had been suffering from bipolar disorder. This disorder is a form of depression. His father had been taking medicine to keep the disease under control, but had stopped taking the medicine a few months before. This was why he was behaving strangely.

Uncle Jack moved in with Josh and his dad. Together they spent a lot of time with Josh's father. His father had started taking the medicine again. Within a few weeks, Josh's dad started to get back to normal.

Josh still had a lot of questions and talked to a school counselor about his father's illness. He learned that although depression can run in families, it did not mean that he would get it. He also found out a lot about bipolar disorder and learned skills to help him cope with his situation at home.

2

WHAT IS DEPRESSION?

Everyone feels sad or "down in the dumps" at times, but the sadness usually goes away. However, for some people, these sad feelings remain for a long while. A person who feels bad for a very long time might have depression.

Depression is a disease that affects a person's moods. Moods are the way a person feels and how he or she expresses those feelings. Someone who suffers from depression may feel sad, angry, irritable, tired, confused, guilty, or worthless. A person who is depressed may lose interest in almost everything he or she used to enjoy.

Depression can cause physical changes in the body, too. A person with depression may have aches and pains and other health problems. Depression also changes the way a person acts. Somebody who is depressed may yell and throw things. He or she may not eat enough or eat too much. This person might have trouble sleeping or feel so tired that he or she stays in bed most of the time. Depression can have a serious effect on a person's life. It can cause problems with school, a job, family, and friends.

Depression is not a weakness or a personality problem. It is an actual disease. It is painful for the person who has it. The disease can also be difficult for the person's family and friends.

The good news is that a person with depression can be helped. There are a number of treatments that a doctor can use to help him or her feel better. There are also things a person with depression can do to get healthier. While there is no one single cure for depression, there is help and there is hope. No one with the disease should suffer alone.

How Many People Suffer From Depression?

Depression can affect people of all ages, races, or religions. Millions of people around the world suffer from depression. Many people who have it do not seek help, so the exact number of people with depression is unknown. But according to a 1999 report by the United States Surgeon General (the country's spokesperson about health issues), forty million Americans suffer from depression. More than three million of those people are children and teenagers. Unfortunately, only fourteen out of the forty million get medical treatment for their depression.

YOUNG PEOPLE AND DEPRESSION

When they are feeling sad, upset, or disappointed, many people—young or old—will say that they are depressed. This does not mean that they are suffering from depression. Sadness and moodiness are normal emotions for young people—especially children and teenagers. But what surprises many people is that bad times for some children and teenagers can be more than just a bad mood or "typical" teenage behavior. In fact, approximately 3.5 million children and teenagers suffer from depression. That is between 10 and 15 percent of all young people. The United States Surgeon General has called depression part of a public health **crisis** for children and teens.

A child or teenager who is depressed may act differently than a depressed adult. Adults suffering from depression are often more sad and quiet. Children and teenagers are more likely to be irritable, angry, and **aggressive.** Depressed young people often sleep and eat more than usual. They have aches and pains that do not get better with treatment.

A young person who is suffering from depression may be able to "snap out of it" for a few hours at a time and have fun before the depressed mood hits again. One of the main signs that a young person may have depression is if he or

When children and teenagers have problems or emotions they need to discuss, they may talk to their parents, teachers, or guidance counselors.

she has been doing worse in school. A drop in grades, poor attendance, or quitting a school activity are all warning signs of depression.

Young people suffering from depression are also much more likely than adults to suffer from another mental disorder. Half of all depressed teens have or have had illnesses such as **anxiety** disorder, social **phobia** (a fear of social situations, people, and new places), or **Attention Deficit Hyperactivity Disorder (ADHD).**

13

Fortunately, as with adults, young people who receive the proper treatment can get better.

WHAT CAUSES DEPRESSION?

Experts do not know exactly what causes depression. Some experts think that some chemicals in the brain get out of balance, resulting in depression. Others believe that it may be hereditary, which means that a person can have it if his or her parent suffers from depression. Some doctors feel that a person's environment and emotions play a large part in developing depression. Today, many experts believe that a combination of these things cause depression. All of these things are called risk factors. By looking at a person's risk factors, a health professional can better understand why the person is depressed. They can then determine what kind of treatment will help.

Brain Chemicals

The brain is a complex organ that sits inside of your skull. It is responsible for controlling body functions that allow you to live. These include breathing, moving, talking, or listening. But the brain is also responsible for your thoughts and feelings.

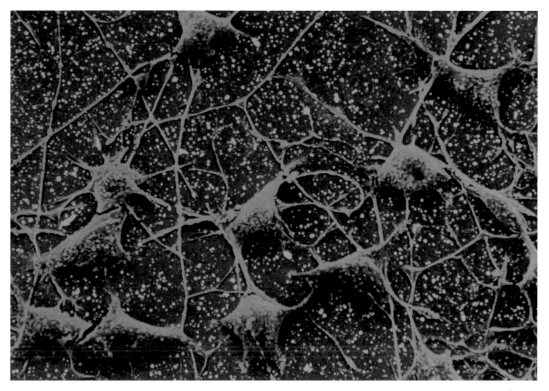

A magnified image of nerve cells.

The brain contains billions of nerve cells. These cells—or neurons—are also found throughout the body. The neurons are responsible for relaying chemical messages back and forth from the brain to different parts of the body. For example, these messages may be from your brain telling you to blink your eyes, or from nerves on your skin telling your brain that something is hot or cold. Each neuron consists of a cell body, an axon, and dendrites. Axons and dendrites are the thin fibers that stick out from the neuron's cell body. Axons send the messages out from one neuron to other neurons. The dendrites bring in messages from other neurons.

Neurons "talk" to each other using chemicals. These special chemicals are called **neurotransmitters**. ("Neuro" refers to something that has to do with the **nervous system** and "transmit" means to sends something.) The neurotransmitters travel from one neuron to another across the gaps that are found between neurons. The neurotransmitters deliver messages to different parts of the brain. The messages cause the brain to have thoughts, emotions, and sensations.

In depression, it is believed that either too much or too little of certain neurotransmitters are sent throughout the brain. A chemical imbalance can lead to depression. Many scientists believe that **serotonin** is one of the brain chemicals related to depression. People who are depressed may have too little serotonin available to "spark" the brain cells that make a person feel good.

Besides neurotransmitters, scientists also believe that **hormones** might play a role in causing depression. Hormones are chemicals that are involved in body functions. These chemicals also affect processes in the brain.

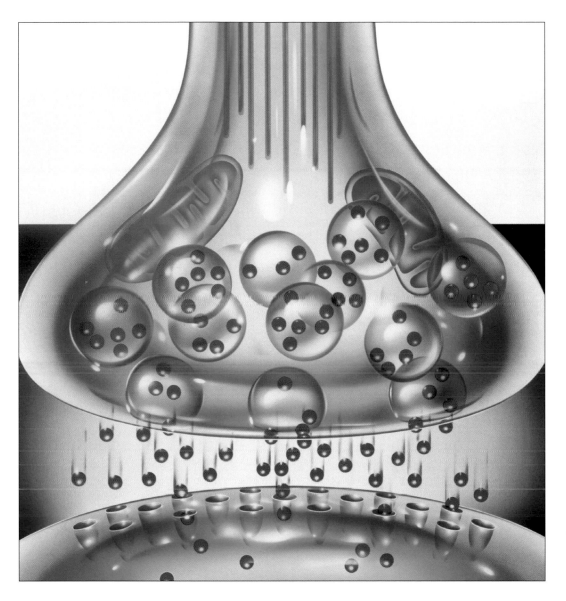

This picture shows neurotransmitters (shown here as red balls) being released from the axon of a neuron. The neurotransmitters travel across the gap toward the end of a dendrite belonging to a separate neuron.

Heredity

Genes are small units in the cells of the body. A child receives or inherits genes from his or her parents. Genes give a person particular characteristics. There are genes for hair color, eye color, and height. There are also genes for diseases. Scientists believe there may be a gene for depression.

Some doctors think depression may be inherited. A parent with depression may pass the gene for depression to his or her child. That child may also eventually develop depression. Research has shown that children of parents with major depression are two to three times more likely than other people to develop the disease. More than half of all people diagnosed with bipolar disorder have a relative who also has some form of depression. Inheriting the gene for depression does not mean that the person will definitely have the disease. However, that person is more likely to become depressed than someone who does not inherit the gene.

Stress

Some experts believe painful or stressful events that happen in a person's environment such as his or her home, job, school or neighborhood, may cause depression. A stressful event can cause a person to feel a sense of loss, hopelessness, or confusion. He or she may also feel sad and lonely. These feelings from the stressful situation could cause depression. Some stressful events that could trigger depression include having a very heavy workload; losing a loved one through death, divorce, or separation; constant family conflict (fighting or arguing a lot); money problems; disappointment after completing a goal (a feeling of

People of all ages can feel stressed at different times in their lives.

"What do I do now?"); major life changes such as job loss or being in a natural disaster; and physical or mental abuse.

Dealing with Emotions

Everybody has emotions. But different people deal with their emotions in different ways. Some types of emotions can lead to depression. How a person deals with different emotions can determine how bad the depression will be and how long the illness will last.

Could You or Someone You Know Suffer from Depression?

If a person answers "yes" to two or more of the following questions, he or she may be suffering from depression. That person should talk to a doctor. Only a health professional can officially determine whether or not a person is suffering from depression.

1. Do I feel down in the dumps or crabby and angry almost all of the time?
2. Have I lost interest in things I used to enjoy?
3. Have I thought about killing myself? (If the answer is "yes," the person needs immediate help no matter how he or she answers the other questions.)
4. Have I been eating too much or not enough?
5. Have I been sleeping too much or not enough?
6. Do I feel tired for no reason?
7. Have I been having trouble concentrating or thinking clearly? Is my work or schoolwork suffering?
8. Do I feel hopeless or worthless?
9. Am I using alcohol or drugs?
10. Do I often have unexplained headaches, stomachaches, or body pains?

Depression can affect people of all ages.

Some people keep emotions like loneliness, anger, sadness, and fear inside. They do not discuss their feelings and do not try to solve the problems causing these emotions. This is unhealthy and can cause depression. Holding in emotions like anger or fear can make a person yell or strike out in anger at other people. This can make others stay away, leading to more loneliness and sadness. A person who worries too much and is always afraid of bad things happening may become depressed. Someone who does not deal with these types of emotions has a higher chance of suffering from depression. People who cope with these feelings in positive ways—by seeking help or talking to family, friends, or medical professionals—have a better of chance of avoiding depression.

Depression can also be linked to **self-esteem.** Self-esteem is the way a person feels about himself or herself. People who have low self-esteem feel bad about themselves. They might not like the way they look or act. They often think that they are no fun or that no one likes them. Many people with low self-esteem feel helpless. They think that they cannot change the things that are making them unhappy or that they will be unhappy forever. People with low self-esteem are more likely to become depressed. Talking to friends, family, counselors, or medical professionals can help people with low self-esteem.

About one-half of people who suffer from depression also have problems with anxiety. Anxiety—or being anxious—involves feelings of nervousness or fear. Everybody feels anxious sometimes. An upcoming exam, performance, or sports game can make a person anxious. Anxiety can be a normal reaction to a situation. But the worries usually do not last very long and do not occur too frequently. Healthy feelings of anxiety normally do not interfere with the rest of a person's life.

Some people, however, experience a lot of anxiety. They worry about many things very often, and may be fearful for no reason. Their anxiety affects their thoughts, moods, and behaviors. Anxiety can also cause physical symptoms such as **fatigue** (extreme tiredness), stomach problems, headaches, dizziness, fidgeting, and a fast heartbeat. Long-term (long-lasting) anxiety is stressful to the body and can contribute to serious physical illness. People whose anxiety gets in the way of their mental or physical health have an anxiety disorder. They may also have feelings of sadness or hopelessness and be suffering from depression, too. Often, a person who is treated for depression finds that his or her anxiety decreases as well.

Physical Illness

Having a physical illness is a possible cause of depression for two reasons. An illness itself can cause changes in the body.

These chemical or physical changes can then lead to depression. Depression is a **symptom** of diseases such as cancer, heart disease, and **Chronic Fatigue Syndrome (CFS).**

The second way illness and depression are linked is through pain, stress, or frustration. A person who is ill might be in a lot of pain. The illness might prevent a person from doing things as well as before he or she was sick. For example, a person with an illness may not be able to walk, talk, go out, or eat normally. The frustration of not being able to do these things can make a person very unhappy. The pain and frustration of physical illness can cause a lot of stress. These stressful feelings can then lead to depression. Treating the physical illness may help relieve some depression.

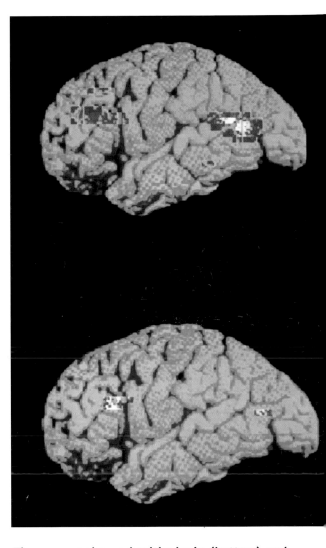

These scans show a healthy brain (bottom) and the brain of a person suffering from depression (top). The red and yellow areas on the depressed brain indicate low brain activity. Chemical imbalances in the brain—which can cause certain types of low brain activity—are involved in depression.

A doctor may also **prescribe** treatment for depression along with the treatment for the illness.

Alcohol and Drug Abuse

Alcohol and drug use is another risk factor for depression. Abusing alcohol or drugs is called substance abuse. Depression and substance abuse often go hand-in-hand. Many alcohol and drug abusers are depressed. Most teenagers who use drugs or alcohol are depressed without knowing it.

Substance abuse is a very serious problem. People who have substance abuse problems—whether or not they are depressed—need immediate help.

Drugs and alcohol change the chemicals in the brain. These chemical changes can lead to depression. Also, a person might abuse drugs and alcohol to try to stop the feelings related to depression. But this does not work. Alcohol and drug use cannot treat depression. Drugs and alcohol can make someone feel differently only for a short while—they do not make problems go away.

In fact, they often make things worse. People suffering from depression and substance abuse need to seek treatment for both the depression and the substance abuse.

TYPES OF DEPRESSION

There are different types of depression. People with different types of depression show various symptoms. A doctor or health professional must examine these symptoms and determine if the person is depressed. The health professional must then determine which type of depression a person is suffering from.

Major Depression

Major depression is a mood disorder that affects one mood—sadness. A doctor may identify a person with major depression if he or she has one of the following symptoms for at least two weeks or longer:

- Feeling sad most of the day, almost everyday
- For most of day every day, a loss of interest in things that he or she used to enjoy; Additionally, the person might show five or more of the following symptoms almost every day.
- A lot of weight gain or weight loss when not dieting, a decrease in appetite, or an increase in appetite
- Not being able to sleep or oversleeping often
- Moving much slower than usual

- Feeling very tired or having no energy
- Feeling unworthy or guilty
- Not being able to think, concentrate, or make decisions
- Constant thoughts about death or **suicide** (killing one's self) with no plan; having a plan to commit suicide or making an attempt to commit suicide.

Bipolar Disorder

Another form of depression is called bipolar disorder. This type of depression used to be called manic depression. Bi means two. Polar refers to things that are opposite. Bipolar disorder is a type of depression that affects two opposite moods: joy and sadness. A person with bipolar has extreme "ups", called mania, and the extreme "downs" of depression. These two moods swing back and forth or go up and down throughout the day or throughout a week, a month, or a year.

Symptoms of mania include feelings of extreme joy or extreme irritability. Manic people may also feel that they can do anything. They may sleep for only two to four hours per night, but still feel rested. Their thoughts may race quickly or rapidly jump from one topic to another. A manic person may be more talkative, speaking faster than usual. Mania may include being easily distracted by unimportant things.

Someone experiencing mania loses touch with reality. As a result, the person may do things that are harmful. A person who is manic may go shopping and spend thousands of dollars without being able to afford it. He or she may also try to do the impossible. For example, somebody in a manic mood could think he or she can fly and will jump out of a window trying to prove it. Periods of mania can be very dangerous.

When the manic period ends, the mood of a person with bipolar disorder can quickly crash into depression. He or she will experience the same symptoms as a person with major depression, including sadness and tiredness. A doctor can only identify a person with bipolar disorder if he or she has both the manic and depressive moods. Bipolar disorder can be treated with medication. About 2.3 million Americans have bipolar disorder.

Seasonal Affective Disorder (SAD)

Another form of depression is seasonal affective disorder (SAD). Seasonal affective disorder usually happens during the seasons of fall and winter. Many people feel better physically and emotionally when there is plenty of sunlight. People with SAD usually feel very sad, tired, irritable, or anxious during the seasons that do not have a lot of sunlight, such as fall

A woman reads a book as she undergoes photo-therapy treatment for SAD. The light screen uses bright light similar to sunlight.

and winter. They may feel the days are dark and dreary. They could overeat, sleep too much, and gain weight.

In the spring, the days get longer and warmer. A person with SAD usually feels better because there is more sunlight. The weight gained during the dark months is usually lost once it gets sunnier and warmer. Treatment for SAD includes sitting in front of a special machine that gives off light that is like sunlight.

Postpartum Depression

Postpartum depression can happen to a woman after she gives birth to a baby. This form of depression affects 15 percent of all new mothers. Although most women are happy to have a new baby, they often have a few days of "baby blues" or sadness after the birth. Postpartum depression, however, lasts for weeks or months after the baby's birth.

A woman with postpartum depression can feel sad, exhausted, irritable, confused, and helpless. She could have trouble concentrating and she may cry a lot. She might worry about her baby most of the time, or she may not want to spend time with the child. A woman with postpartum depression may think of hurting her baby or herself.

A new mother may experience postpartum depression. Women who have this problem should seek medical help since the condition is treatable.

Women with postpartum depression often feel guilty and depressed because they feel like they should be very happy about the new baby, but they cannot. Having postpartum depression does not mean that a woman does not love her newborn baby. This type of depression is an illness that can usually be treated. Any woman who feels this way for more than a week after giving birth should seek help. She needs to tell her doctor about her feelings so her doctor can help her. Treatment for postpartum depression usually involves medication and time.

Dysthymia

Dysthymia is a form of depression that may be more difficult to recognize than major depression. Dysthymia can make a person feel "dragged down" or "dulled" most days. A doctor can identify an adult with dysthymia if the person has been sad almost all day and almost every day for at least two years. A doctor may recognize a teenager or a child with dysthymia, if he or she has a sad or irritable mood almost every day for at least one year. A person with dysthymia also would have to have at least two or more of the following symptoms: poor appetite or overeating; problems sleeping or oversleeping; low energy; not being able to think or make decisions; or feelings of hopelessness.

Suicide

Some people become so depressed that they think about or attempt to kill themselves. Depression is a major cause of suicide. About thirty thousand people commit suicide in the United States every year. Hundreds of thousands of others try to kill themselves, but do not succeed. Many people who attempt suicide are young people. In fact, suicide is the number three cause of death for teenagers, behind automobile accidents and murder. In some cases, if the depression is treated and the person is able to talk to trained professionals, there is a chance that suicide can be prevented.

What You Can Do

A person thinking about committing suicide might display these behaviors:

- Threatening to commit suicide or talking about suicide
- Appearing obsessed (overly concerned) with death
- Writing poems, essays, or stories, or drawing pictures that refer to death
- Showing a very obvious and serious change in personality or appearance
- Acting strangely or unreasonably
- Feeling very guilty or shameful
- Changing eating or sleeping habits
- Showing a bad change in school or work performance
- Giving away belongings

If someone talks about killing himself or herself, that person needs help immediately. If someone you know displays any of the habits listed above, you should speak with a trusted adult as soon as possible. Even if it may seem like someone is just joking about suicide, it is important to talk to an adult. If you are with a person who is thinking about suicide or is trying to commit suicide, try to stay with the person until he or she gets help. Call 911 immediately—especially if the person is in danger or if you are in danger. You should also call an adult you trust right away. You could save a life.

3

THE HISTORY OF DEPRESSION

Depression was recognized thousands of years ago by the oldest civilizations. Egyptians wrote about it, and built a temple that appears to have served as a hospital for people suffering from mental illness. Angry or troublemaking gods were thought to be the cause, so prayers and rituals to them were an important treatment. Ancient Greeks and Romans also recognized that people could go through difficult emotional periods. They called deep sadness melancholia, and unusually strong happiness mania—terms that are still in use today. Like the Egyptians, they blamed the gods for mental illness.

However, it was a Greek physician named Hippocrates who, much later (around 300 B.C.E.), proposed a scientific explanation. He thought that illnesses were caused by an imbalance of four substances, or humors, in the body. The humors were blood, yellow bile, black bile, and phlegm. Hippocrates believed that an excess of black bile made people sad.

This engraving was created in the 1500s. Many believe that it is a representation of the thoughts and feelings associated with sadness or melancholy. In this engraving, melancholy is called "Melencholia."

As scientists and physicians continued to study the behavior of mentally ill people, a scientific explanation gradually developed. A book called *Anatomy of Melancholy,* published by Robert Burton in 1621, was a start, and other people like Jean-Pierre Fairet in France (in the mid 1800s), and Emil Kraepelin (in the early 1900s) described symptoms of the main mental illnesses known today. Like Hippocrates, Kraepelin emphasized that mental illness was related to a person's inner chemistry. The famous German psychiatrist Sigmund Freud, who lived at the same time as Kraepelin, thought instead that childhood events and relationships among family members determined how a person felt as an adult. (We now know that both ideas are right.)

Before the 1900s, there were very few useful treatments for depression, and society frowned upon mentally ill people. Many were locked up in prisons or left to wander as homeless rejects without help. But Dorthea Lynde Dix helped to change that. She was an American woman from the 1800s who suffered a serious depression, but recovered under the kind treatment of a Quakers family she stayed with in England. The Quakers had created special group homes where mentally ill people were taken care of and treated kindly. Dorthea Dix devoted her life to creating similar places in the United States, called

Some institutions provided comfortable furniture and living areas for patients. This photograph was taken in 1900 in a mental hospital in Boston.

asylums, (asylum means a safe refuge). Sadly, after her death, the asylums gradually became horrible places because of overcrowding and abuse of the residents. Many improvements have been made now, but even today, some so-called "mental hospitals" have those problems.

In the last hundred years, a number of treatments has made it possible for most depressed people to lead normal lives.

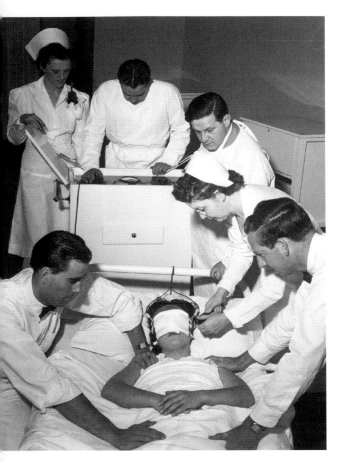

For many years, electroshock therapy has been used to treat mental disorders.

Some of the earlier treatments were harsh, like strong doses of drugs or electric shocks. These shocks made a person become unconscious for a while. When they woke up they felt less depressed. In desperate cases, areas of the brain were damaged to stop the mental illness.

Another approach involved talking to a specially trained doctor, counselor, or therapist. Psychoanalysis, was a series of meetings in which the patient would relax on a couch and speak about anything that came to mind. Sigmund Freud was a big supporter of psychoanalysis. Some doctors would hypnotize a patient, which helped them talk about things they could not or did not want to remember. The doctor then helped figure out how thoughts and memories might be causing the person's mental illness, and how to overcome them.

Today, the treatments just described are still used, but with changes and improvements. Psychoanalysis is less popular, but psychotherapy (also called "talk therapy") has replaced it as an important part of helping a depressed person. It gives the person a chance to explain situations at home, school, or work that are upsetting. A therapist listens and makes helpful suggestions. But the main way in which depression is treated today in the United States is with antidepressant medication and psychotherapy together.

The first antidepressant medicine was discovered by accident when it was noticed that a drug being used for another illness could change the mood of depressed patients. Scientists also had discovered that brain cells made neuro-transmitters that could influence a person's mood and behavior. Starting in the 1950s, drugs were created that could change the amount of neurotransmitters in a person's brain.

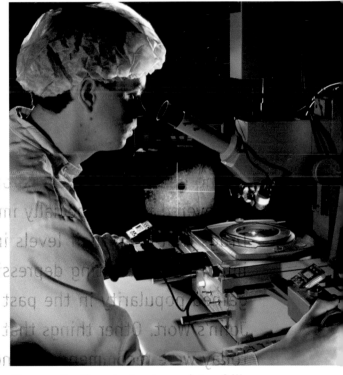

New medications to treat a variety of illnesses are being studied and tested around the world.

As researchers learn more about the human brain and how it works, more progress can be made in treating—and possibly preventing—illnesses like depression.

The neurotransmitters serotonin and norepinephrine were discovered to be especially important to feelings of happiness. Drugs that keep their levels in the brain high are now very important in treating depression. Herbal remedies have also gained popularity in the past several decades, particularly St. John's Wort. Other things that are helpful to a depressed person today were recommended hundreds of years ago, like a healthy diet, exercise, sufficient sleep, and a healthy environment. All of these help to give a person the vitamins, minerals, and oxygen that we now know are important for keeping the brain (and the body's other organs) functioning properly.

Because medicines and therapy still cannot prevent or cure all cases of depression, research and exploration of new ideas continues. Some psychotherapists are emphasizing the need for more interaction among caring friends and family to help keep a person from becoming depressed. Having a pet has been shown to greatly help depressed people feel better and be able to function again. The role of genetics and of other chemicals and organs in the body are being studied for explanations and new treatments.

Famous People Who Suffered from Depression

Today, it is much more common to hear about people who have dealt with depression. Many well-known people have spoken about their depression. They encourage others to seek help. Here is a list of some people who suffered from depression. Despite their illness, these people were able to accomplish a great deal.

Abraham Lincoln, sixteenth United States President
Charles Dickens, author
Kristy McNichol, actress
Delta Burke, actress
Carrie Fisher, writer and actress
Emily Dickinson, poet

4

LIVING WITH DEPRESSION

Thanks to advances in medicine and health research, depression can be treated. There are many different ways to help someone who is depressed. The first step is recognizing that there is a problem. Someone who is suffering from depression may not even realize that he or she has a real illness.

Only a doctor or health professional can officially determine whether or not a person is suffering from depression. It is good for people to notice the signs of depression, but they need to see a professional for treatment. Although help is widely available, according to the National Institute of Mental Health, only about one third of all people with depression seek treatment. Depression may make a person feel too tired, too sick, or too hopeless to seek help. Some people have a hard time admitting that they need help. People who are suffering from depression might need a family member or friend to help them get the help they need.

A family doctor or other health professional can help a person with depression find the expert that will work best for him or her. It is important to see an expert that under-stands depression. Children or teens may need to see a professional who works mainly with young people who suffer from depression.

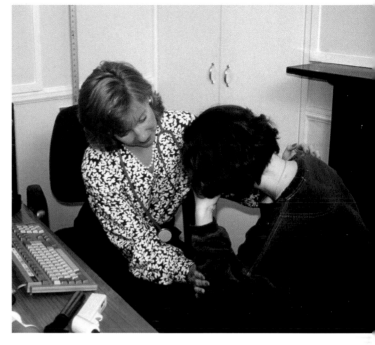

Depending upon what the problem might be, a general physician might prescribe a specific treatment, or send the patient to a specialist. Specialists are doctors who focus on specific types of medical problems.

How does a doctor or health professional decide if a person has depression? A patient who might be suffering from depression needs to tell the health professional about how he or she is feeling. These would include bad moods, aches and pains, or other illnesses. A patient is also asked for a family medical history. This includes talking about any medical problems that the patient or his or her parents, brothers, or sisters have had. Physical examinations may be performed to check if a physical illness could be causing problems.

Experts Who Treat Depression

Many different health professionals can help a person who is suffering from depression.

- A family doctor or general physician can identify depression, and order medication to treat it. A family doctor can also recommend other experts or doctors who specialize in depression.
- Psychiatrists are doctors who recognize depression, order medication to treat it, and give talk **therapy.**
- Psychologists can identify depression and give talk therapy.
- Psychiatric Nurse Practitioners are registered nurses who can recognize depression, order medication, and give talk therapy.
- Clinical Social Workers can identify depression and give talk therapy.

After the expert asks questions and performs a physical exam, he or she may come up with a **diagnosis.** A diagnosis is the identification of a disease by examining symptoms. To diagnose mental health diseases such as depression and bipolar disorder, experts use a book called the *Diagnostic and Statistical Manual of Mental Disorders,* or *DSM* for short. The *DSM* lists hundreds of mental illnesses. Each has a description and a list of symptoms. If a patient's symptoms fit the description of depression, the health professional will tell the person what form of depression he or she is suffering from. Experts also rely on their past experience with depression patients. Once a type of depression is determined, treatment can begin.

TREATMENTS FOR DEPRESSION

Depression is a serious disease. If it is left untreated, the depression could become worse. There are a number of treatments that a doctor or expert could use to help someone suffering from depression.

Talk Therapy or Psychotherapy

This treatment involves talking to an expert about one's feelings, behaviors, and problems. The therapist can help a person learn how to talk about problems. They will also discuss how to solve problems in a healthy way. Talk therapy is a good way to help a person learn to change behaviors that are not healthy. It also teaches someone how to accept and deal with his or her illness. Talk therapy can take place between just the person and the therapist. Or, it can be done in a group where people who have depression share their feelings and problems. Sometimes, it can include family members, so that the family may learn how to understand and help.

Counseling by a trained professional can help someone who is experiencing problems.

Two of the most common kinds of talk therapy used for depression are cognitive behavior therapy (CBT) and interpersonal therapy. Some experts use both CBT and interpersonal therapy. They believe that a combination of approaches is most effective.

Experts who use CBT believe that people who suffer from depression have learned to see themselves, the world, and their future as negative or unhappy. Cognitive behavior therapy helps a person change his or her thoughts and behaviors to more positive ones. Over time, these new positive thoughts and actions can help relieve stress and lift the person's mood.

Interpersonal therapy deals with the relationships that a person has with others. Experts who use interpersonal therapy help people communicate with other people. The person undergoing therapy learns to understand people better and learns how to express his or her feelings in a clearer way. This helps the person get along better with family and friends. These skills help a person suffering from depression solve problems with others. He or she usually becomes more comfortable and feels connected with the world.

The more somebody shares with the expert the better talk therapy will work. The patient should try not to feel ashamed

Counseling by a trained professional can help someone who is experiencing problems.

or embarrassed about talking to a therapist. An expert listens without judging. A therapist is there to help.

Medication

Medication can be taken to help treat depression. These medicines are called antidepressants. Of the 14 million patients treated for depression in the United States each year, about 80 percent take antidepressant medication. Medicines help to balance a person's brain chemicals. Only a doctor can order or **prescribe** the medication.

Antidepressants can be taken as a pill or as a liquid. There are many types of antidepressants, and the doctor decides which type and how much is needed. Some medications to treat depression include Prozac, Zoloft, Paxil, Celexa, and Luvox. These are selective serotonin reuptake inhibitors (SSRI's).

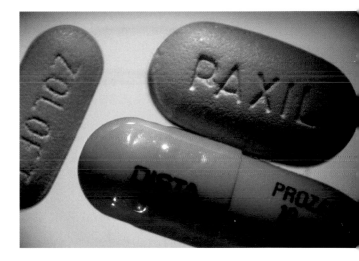

Doctors today prescribe many different types of antidepressants for different patients.

SSRI's help the brain absorb the chemical serotonin. Serotonin can help a person feel better. However, these medications are not "happy pills." They do not immediately make a person happy.

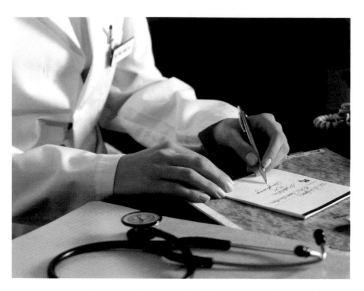

When certain medications are not working, doctors may increase or decrease the dose or try a different type of medication.

Other medication such as Wellbutrin and Serzone are called atypical anti-depressants. They also work on brain chemicals and are used to treat depression. Lithium is the medication most often prescribed for bipolar disorder. Lithium helps prevent mania. It can also work on depression, although some people need to take an antidepressant along with lithium.

It can take four to six weeks for the depression medication to work correctly. This is because medication needs time to build up to a level where it can help. After four to six weeks, the doctor will likely ask questions to see if the medicine is working. The doctor might increase or decrease the dose (amount) or change the type of medicine. Sometimes a person has to try a second or third medication before finding the one that works the best. Depending upon the type of depression he or she is suffering from, a person may need to take medicine for a few months or for many years.

Many experts feel that treating depression with both medication and talk therapy can be the best way to help someone feel better. Medication can help a person think more clearly and feel well enough to then make the other lifestyle changes that are needed.

Electroconvulsive Therapy (ECT)

This therapy is also called electro-shock treatment. It can treat depression by using a very small dose of electricity to cause changes in the brain. Doctors are very careful about the amount of electricity used. Too much can permanently damage the brain, so only trained professionals should perform this type of therapy. ECT is used only if talk therapy and medication are not working. It is used mostly on people with **severe** depression who need help so that they do not harm themselves or others.

Side Effects

....

Taking certain medications can cause side effects. These are feelings of sickness or pain. There is always a chance of experiencing side effects when taking any medication. A person taking medication for depression might feel these side effects: headaches, a dry mouth, **nausea,** being nervous, dizziness or fainting, digestive problems, sleep problems, feeling tired, allergic reactions. Not everyone taking the medication will experience these problems. It is important for the patient to tell the doctor about any side effects that he or she is feeling. Some side effects could lessen or go away, or the doctor may decide to give a different medication.

Hospitalization

A person suffering from depression may need to stay in a hospital. People who do not respond to traditional treatments are often hospitalized. People who are suicidal are also hospitalized, where they can be monitored carefully. Some people suffering from depression are admitted to a general hospital and treated on a psychiatric ward (department). Others may enter a mental health institution for treatment. The health professionals at these places specialize in mental illness and can provide the care, supervision, and therapy that a seriously depressed person needs. Hospital stays can last from days to months, depending on the illness.

Coping with Depression

To cope means to deal with a situation. There are four ways a person can cope with depression: education, treatment, prevention, and support.

Education. Learning about depression can help someone understand and cope with the disease. There are many good books available for people of all ages in libraries and bookstores. The Internet also has plenty of Web sites that offer information. It can also be helpful to get answers to questions directly from someone who knows about depression, such as a counselor or a clergy member. There are also telephone hotline numbers to call. However, it is important to remember that nothing can take the place of an official diagnosis from a health profession.

Treatment. There are many kinds of treatments that can help someone suffering from depression. Going to therapy sessions, taking the medication that has been prescribed, and following doctor's advice are all important parts of a treatment plan. A person has a better chance of becoming healthy if he or she follows through on treatment.

Prevention. In some cases, depression cannot be prevented. It is a chemical imbalance that needs to be fixed. But people can do things to prevent depression from getting worse. People who suffer from depression often feel like their lives are not in their control. They may not realize that there are steps that they can take to feel better. A person who practices stress management skills can feel happier and healthier. These skills can help a person cope with and may prevent severe depression.

Stress Management Skills

Thinking positive thoughts. A person who is depressed may think bad or negative thoughts like "I am no good" or "I cannot do it." These thoughts can lead to feelings of hopelessness, fear,

Learning to play an instrument or joining a band can be a fun way to feel good about yourself.

or anxiety. That person should try to change his or her thoughts to positive ones like "I many not be good at everything, but I am good at art, a good athlete, a good friend, or a good person." These thoughts can lead to feelings of happiness, pride, and hope. Even if it seems a little strange at first, saying good things about one's self can become a good habit and raise self-esteem.

There are many ways that a person can build good self-esteem and feel better about his or her life. Helping someone else, such as reading to senior citizens in a nursing home, helping children with homework, making dinner for your family, or saying something kind to a classmate, are all positive activities. To build self-esteem, a person should do things that he or she enjoys, such as taking part in hobbies, sports, or other games. It is helpful to do something creative like writing a poem, a song, or story, or learning to play an instrument or painting. Good self-esteem includes setting sensible goals and making a plan on how to attain those goals. Expressing affection in appropriate ways such as saying, "I love you," "I like you," giving someone a hug, or cuddling an animal can help a person feel better. It is also important to keep a sense of humor. Laughter releases stress and makes a person feel good.

Getting enough sleep and rest. Resting the body and mind is a healthful way to cope with stress. When the body is resting, it can store up energy to use later. If a person does not get enough sleep or rest, he or she is more likely to feel unwell.

Eating right and exercising. Eating the right foods in healthy amounts can help a person stay strong and feel well. Healthful foods such as whole grains, fruits, vegetables, and lean meats contribute to wellness. Too much junk food, sugar, or caffeine can make a person feel bad and cause poor health.

Exercising helps get the heart and blood pumping at a steady rate, which helps keep the body healthy. It also causes the brain to release chemicals that make a person feel good. Even a small

Part of staying healthy includes exercising or doing some sort of physical activity.

amount of exercise, such as a walk around the neighborhood or dancing to a favorite song, can relieve stress and lift a person's mood. A person who is suffering from depression may have a hard time getting moving at first, so he or she may need encouragement. As the person exercises more, his or her energy will likely increase and it will become easier and more enjoyable.

Expressing feelings in appropriate ways. Everyone feels worried, angry, sad, or lonely sometimes. People handle these feelings in different ways. Some people suffering from depression keep their feelings inside. This causes more pain and makes them even more alone. Other people yell, fight, or throw things. This does not help the feelings go away, and it can be harmful to themselves or to others. Expressing feelings appropriately involves dealing with the feelings so that a person feels better. How does someone express his or her feelings appropriately? When feelings of anger, sadness, or worry surface, deep breathing can help. Taking slow, deep breaths relaxes the body and helps a person to feel calm. Then, he or she can let feelings out without losing control. Talking to a trusted friend or family member can help release emotions in a positive way. Discussing problems with a health

Many people undergo group therapy to discuss problems or feelings that they might have in common. Group therapy can help a person make new friends or help a person feel better about what they are going through.

professional can also be very effective. Writing in a journal or crying (for a short period of time) can let feelings out when a person is alone.

What You Can Do

Here are some things that you can say to someone you know who may be suffering from depression:

"I am here for you." Just being available to listen lets the person know you care.

"Here is the contact information (name, phone number, or Web site address) of an organization that might help." Some people are not aware that there are resources for people who suffer from depression.

"I think we should tell an adult about this because you need more help than I can give you." This is very important if you are a young person dealing with someone who may be depressed.

There are things that you should not say or do to people who might be depressed:

"You will snap out of it." "Lighten up." "It is all in your head." Depression is a real disease that often requires treatment.

Doing or saying nothing. Do not ignore a person who seems depressed just because you feel uncomfortable or do not know what to say. This will only make the person feel more alone and can cause more serious problems.

Getting Support

Getting support means getting help from someone who listens and understands. A supporter can be a friend, relative, counselor, or doctor. A person who is suffering from depression may find it hard to ask for support, but it is very important for him or her not to try to cope with the disease alone.

Sometimes a group of people meets to give each other support. Support groups provide an opportunity to share information, discuss problems, and communicate with others who understand what a person is going through. Attending a support group can help a person suffering from depression feel less alone. Many hospitals and mental health care providers offer support groups for depression.

Resilience

Being resilient means being able to "bounce back" from changes or disappointments. Resilience helps a person cope with depression. With education, treatment, stress management skills, and support, a person can feel that he or she has more control over the disease. Instead of feeling helpless and hopeless, a person who learns to cope with the ups and downs of life will be better able to cope with—and may even overcome—depression.

Here are some ways for a person to be resilient:

- A person should not lose sight of the big picture. This means that a person should try not to worry too much about small things. When things go wrong, it is important to remind one's self that things will not be bad or wrong forever.

- It is important to find what makes a person happy. Whether it is listening to music, reading a book, working out, sewing, or hiking, a person should engage in these activities a lot. A favorite activity can lift a person out of a bad mood.

- Spending time with people who are positive is good. People should make sure the company they keep makes them better, happier people. It is not good to be surrounded by people who are too negative.

- Everybody should realize that change and disappointment are facts of life. Everyone has good times and bad times. It is important to be able to handle both.

- It is healthy to learn to appreciate the good things in one's life—even the small things. Keeping a positive view on life is essential to good mental health.

The support of family, friends, and health professionals can help a person cope with depression and other medical disorders.

Depression can be a difficult and painful disease. The good news is that people suffering from depression can be helped. Just because a person suffers from depression does not mean that he or she cannot have a long and happy life. Today depression is talked about more openly and there are many effective treatments. Depression is not something to be ashamed of, and it does not have to be handled alone.

GLOSSARY

aggressive—Being very forceful and willing to fight or argue.

anxiety—Feelings of nervousness, worry, or fear.

Attention Deficit Hyperactivity Disorder (ADHD)—A medical condition that involves behavioral disorders. Someone with ADHD might have problems with their attention span, activity level, or behavior.

Chronic Fatigue Syndrome (CFS)—A medical condition that involves being tired most of the time.

crisis—An emergency.

diagnose—To determine what is making a person sick.

fatigue—Extreme tiredness.

heredity—The passing on of traits from parents to their children.

hormones—Chemicals that are involved in body functions.

nausea—A sick feeling in the stomach.

nervous system—The body system that includes the brain, spinal cord, and nerves.

neurotransmitters—Chemicals that carry messages across gaps between nerve cells.

phobia—A fear of something.

prescribe—To order something to be used for a medical treatment. A doctor prescribes medication for a patient.

psychiatrist—A doctor who studies the mind and the ways people behave. Psychiatrists can diagnose disorders, offer therapy, and prescribe medication for people with mental disorders.

psychologist—A scientist who studies the mind and the ways people behave. Most psychologist can diagnose mental disorders and offer therapy.

self-esteem—The way a person feels about himself for herself.

serotonin—A brain chemical related to depression.

severe—Very serious.

suicide—The act of killing one's self on purpose.

symptom—A sign that indicates the presence of a disease or illness.

therapy—Treatment for a problem.

FIND OUT MORE

ORGANIZATIONS

American Academy of Child & Adolescent Psychiatry (AACAP)

3615 Wisconsin Avenue NW, Washington, D.C. 20016

1-800-333-7636

www.aacap.org

AACAP is a national professional medical association that researches, evaluates, diagnoses, and treats children with mental, behavioral and developmental disorders.

Depression and Bipolar Support Alliance (DBSA)

730 N. Franklin Street, Suite 501, Chicago, Illinois 60610

1-800-826-3632

www.dbsalliance.org

The DBSA is a nonprofit organization that educates people about depression and bipolar disorder.

National Alliance for the Mentally Ill (NAMI)

Colonial Place Three, 2107 Wilson Blvd., Suite 300

Arlington, VA 22201

1 -800-950-NAMI (1-800-950-6264)

www.nami.org

The NAMI is a nonprofit, organization that works by providing education, supporting and funding research, and advocating for people with serious mental illnesses.

HOTLINES
National Hopeline Network
1-800-SUICIDE (1-800-784-2433)
You can call if someone is having thoughts of death or suicide.

Girls and Boys Town National Hotline
1-800-448-3000
This is a crisis and resource referral service that is available twenty-four hours a day, seven days a week.

Covenant House Nineline
1-800-999-9999
This is a twenty-four-hour, toll free crisis hotline for troubled youths and their families.

BOOKS
American Medical Association. *Essential Guide to Depression*. New York: Pocket Books,1998.

Cobain, Bev. *When Nothing Matters Anymore: A Survival Guide For Depressed Teens*. Minneapolis, MN: Freespirit Publishing, 1998.

Gold, Susan Dudley. *Bipolar Disorder and Depression*. Berkeley Heights, NJ: Enslow Publishers, 2000.

Lennard-Brown, Sarah. *Stress & Depression*. Austin, TX: Raintree Steck-Vaughn, 2001.

Miller, Jeffrey A. *The Childhood Depression Sourcebook*. New York: McGraw-Hill / Contemporary Books, 1999.

Peacock, Judith. *Depression*. Mankato, MN: LifeMatters, 2000.

Wallerstein, Claire. *Depression*. Chicago, IL: Heinemann Library, 2003.

WEB SITES

The Center for Mental Health Services (CMHS)
http://www.mentalhealth.org/cmhs

Covenant House—For Kids
http://www.covenanthouse.org/nineline/kid.html

Girls and Boys Town
http://www.girlsandboystown.org

GOAL! Go On And Live!
http://www.goonandlive.com

National Mental Health Association—Childhood Depression Awareness Day
http://www.nmha.org/children/green/index.cfm

INDEX

ABOUT THE AUTHOR

Jennifer Rozines Roy is the author of more than twenty books, including three for Benchmark Books. A former Gifted & Talented teacher, she holds a B.S. in psychology and an M.A. in elementary education. Ms. Roy has also worked with children with emotional special needs. She lives in upstate New York with her husband Gregory and son Adam.